Insomnia In Flowers

Stella Vinitchi Radulescu

Plain View Press
P. O. 42255
Austin, TX 78704

plainviewpress.net
sb@plainviewpress.net
1-512-441-2452

Copyright Stella Vinitchi Radulescu 2008. All rights reserved.
ISBN: 978-0-911051-29-2
Library of Congress Number: 2008941452

Cover art: *Silhouette*, by Marie-Thérèse Pent - Cunningham.

Acknowledgments

Thanks to the editors of publications in which the following poems first appeared: "Mozart's Requiem" and "The Voice I Don't Have" in *Shade 2006* (*Anthology, Four Way Books*), "Spelling Loud" in *Louisville Review*, "Before Dawn" in *Seneca Review*, "Sunset" in *Sulphur River Review*, "Modigliani's Red" in *Plainsongs Review*, "Learning the Map of the World" in *Istanbul Literature Review*, "A Process in the Weather of the Heart" in *Tupelo Press Poetry Project*, "Stars Are Like Children" in *Visions*.

"Sunset" and "Before Dawn" also appeared in *Self Portrait in Blue*, a chapbook published by March Street Press. My thanks to Robert Bixby.

My sincerest gratitude to David Dodd Lee for his valuable editorial assistance and untiring support of this work.

To my parents

In memoriam

Contents

Spelling Loud	7
As Everything Takes Its Place	8
The Storm In Its Way The Skeleton	9
March Afternoon Stores Open Late	10
Scream	11
The Voice I Don't Have	12
Letter To Someone I Know	13
Hard To Imagine You	14
Temptation	15
French Lesson In The Garden	16
Stars Are Like Children	17
Better Times On Morgue Street	18
Past Present	20
Modigliani's Red	21
Learning The Map Of The World	22
1955	23
Mozart's Requiem	24
Burning Wood As We Talk	25
Rough Winter, Cold Meals	26
History	27
Life Syndrome	28
Mouth Without Face	29
Berryman Style	30
The Orange Long Tail Story	31
Gravity	32
News From My Backyard	33
Before Dawn	35
In Small Waves	36
Deep Blue	37
Imagine	38
Playing Ophelia	39
Blues	40
The Smell Of Snow Reminds	41
Sushi Bar	42
Five Fingers And No Stars	43
Vallejo's Black Heralds	44
Lake Triptych	45
What Remains	46
Wild Geese	47
Sunday No Mail	48
Like Night And Day	49

The Long Hour	50
Civility	51
The Day I Missed	52
When Blue Goes Wrong	53
Insomnia In Flowers	54
Winter Talk	56
Roots Go Beyond The Sky	59
Love At Dusk Or How To Deal With Bad Weather	60
Winter Talk (2)	61
Sweet Amnesia	62
Here Again In The Mist	63
A Process In The Weather Of The Heart	64
That Piece Of Art Next To The Snow	66
Daily Green	67
It Takes A Song	68
Sunday No Mail (2)	69
On Turtles And Death	70
The Red Window	73
I Am Not The Rainbow	74
Sunset	75
Fish Scales	76
If Nowhere	77
Intermission	78
About the Author	79

Spelling Loud

there is a crisp sound in the air
                                earth moving

a day going on

tea sugar on the table
violet sky in somebody's eyes
                          a room
in the room
my flesh in yours   thank you mother

thanks for taking me back   for the fresh leaves
the language I speak once a year when the sun

digs you out   cherry trees in blossom again
rehearsing a new death

spelling loud your silence
                             a short yes
flowers for teeth

teeth for flowers

As Everything Takes Its Place

as everything takes its place
on the map
a flock of wild geese peels off the sky
in Ashbery's convex mirror   smell
of resurrection   there is no time to recuperate

Time

I keep gathering parts of my body

just in case

*

the world is mathematics multiply my soul
with a couple of stars

the engine

the happening   distant murmur of life
not now
not yet maybe tomorrow maybe

light-years away

The Storm In Its Way The Skeleton

the storm in its way the skeleton smells of roses

egg rolls chinese food

late dinner under one star   drops of rain

the contortionist in his final stage pushing out

bones

flooding on the news the storm approaches we are

way down we pose as dead

we skip this line how come nothing

could kill a rose

March Afternoon Stores Open Late

maybe it was March afternoon stores
open late
the eclipse
tall trees I don't remember their names my childhood
a raging thirst

lost in the dense motionless woods the big black eye
above
I have killed the bird
No no that was before   a wet stain on the map
I was wearing my blue chaussettes and a sweater from France

since then the blood dried up   smell of urine
in the hallway   rats
too much dust
one wall not two think about
if so
I could have died sooner

Scream

I went too far, too far in the woods. The tree
was there, the body hanging
from a branch.

It was yesterday, I was looking for God.

Free from gravity, his legs in the wind
right, left...
a creepy balance between shadows and light.

Too far on Earth, too far into night... I touched
the corpse, it went away in flames
and dust.

He is still here in the declining moon some words would fit
his skull

And I was scared, the scream
took my whole body with it, I thought I was flying...

But no, there I found myself stuck on the ground
from scream to scream building
an altar of silence.

The Voice I Don't Have

1.
The voice I don't have is the voice I want,
yours,
broken in pieces, spread out on the floor, hot shower
along my spine...

Your voice, star, trembling at the edge.

2.
And yours,
tall man with the afternoon light in your hair,
separating humans from gods,

one finger from the other...
voice that roars when the music stops,
the damp, the need to open the window,

your voice,
little dead mother, they nailed your coffin,
lashed the night,

they nailed and nailed until something went wrong,
sounds returned to their place
and merged into one word...

Letter To Someone I Know

September night far east on the street
a small boutique still open dresses five
dollars a piece

Policemen in dark uniforms
keeping people on leash dogs
were expensive

It was supposed to rain
late fall to be
I should have stopped right there the hours

But nobody wanted my tears
or I should go ahead and change the story
buy a dress

Leave the country
I am writing to you all this now about our
forgotten lives what we then didn't

Understand our immortality
minutes away
did we

Hard To Imagine You

hard to imagine you walking   the street   joyful
return
america america and the crow

why not to ask questions as we used to do   short days
we didn't even come to the beginning

the handful of seeds my father
threw on the field   the Unicorn   mirror
scavenger with red eyes

and whom should I call father

I can hear the yellow track
early
city workers came with their big hands to clean up the town

Temptation

1.
horses in a dream the rain doesn't stop   saints with their sacred
books reading to the stars

horses   get involved the story of life why not run away why
not come back nothing starts here but horses

2.
in a dream with horses

the rain doesn't stop   saints with no books reading the mind you
in a dream

history of words the word for rain the word for horse something seen
/ heard
something to be cast

as blue as racing the time

French Lesson In The Garden

peel the onion   layer after layer after layer
of white

words won't hurt you as the first snow
comes again from Villon hell

roses with long necks swans floating at dawn

democracy needs more poppies
more red

pause   café crème   between two leaves of grass

yellow comes by surprise like Christ
with a cut off ear

Stars Are Like Children

it was so hot I couldn't open my eyes

a stair   the armchair   universal care for poets he said

in time of war

it should be prose

it was hard to listen or follow the road

not a road

but five fingers diminishing to one

it's enough that's all

I heard from his perspective

under the stars —

stars are like children

playing with us

sky was a joke in our late conversation

a man lightning his blue cigars

with Stevens' tie

Better Times On Morgue Street

> *We existed within ourselves alone.*
> Edgar Allan Poe

remembering the cold   off white   crisp
in our summer heat
they blink in the dark they are not yet muted

nor asleep

same body language

there are dreams all over the wall spiders
and exotic palms climb the hour

dressed in a long milky robe I move toward you

on this tune of smoke

*

he forgot to take his hat

she forgot the lipstick pale as a star

undressed in the mirror   but

on the other side there is plenty of time

nights and days to be returned

footprints of life

*

crows know better the cloning
I could be inside   a thought already freed

floors gradually removed
new species

and the heart follows broad patterns
of disappearance

*

who talks in trees in waves in tongues

a noise like long awaited wings

memory eats from my hands

it licks the window

claws the heart   human

emptiness

who knows the price

*

open area for you to invent the speech
of love

from almost nothing that exists   pleasure
and pain   not even a casket dropped for us

to be wept or hailed

Past Present

I should have come at night   rain and leaves   I should have told you
the truth about the burgundy sky the remote village

top of the mountains the man who wouldn't stop saying
cara mia

he hung up and I have lost track of those days   days like small figurines
who broke them all

some people were riding camels in the sky
some were asleep

viciously late
irreversible

it happens now he talks   hangs up again   I should have
picked up the phone   so many wounded sounds so much you are

the past with its long tail
of lies

Modigliani's Red

1.
Present into past. *A small sky vanishes*
like an old spot on the wall.

I stand in front of the sun, walk between lines,
I touch the air with my lips: bruises, bruises...
Modigliani's red over my face.

2.
Past into present. Space into time.
My parents came a long, long way only to be
The desert I can't hold in my hands.

Am I searching for something to find or to lose?
Wildly sad, diffused, beautiful...
A tactile absence, a virtual blue screen
Withdrawn from human eyes on which only once...

Learning The Map Of The World

1.
we were naked
on naked unlit streets
young and old not knowing our age

yet knowing the fear that was overgrown
with the roses

2.
we were in school learning the map of the world
just at the right scale:
bodies surrounded with walls of deep water
and fiery dogs

but sadness felt so good in the warm rain

and we were happy to break our lives into small pieces
and give them away
to unhappy strangers
forgotten

coffins nailed on sunny streets with no sound

1955

To scream once it takes seconds;
to scream twice it takes hours,
to scream for ever obliterates time.

Nothing wears black watch plaid shirt for special occasions

like when the father was taken away,
melted snow dripped from the gutters

spring was about to come...

*

And we still have these words —
bare bones and barbed wired in our own souls,
lost imagination

outdated chromosomes drying up
on the plate.

Dark pleasure. Lips in a cage start singing the anthem.

Who are you at the beginning
of the century
to be asking questions about happiness?

Mozart's Requiem

> *An ear, cut off, is listening.*
> Paul Celan

They have lived a stone life, a star life, a rat life,
tears wiped out by the Siberian wind, packages wrapped
in despair,
moved from prison to prison, from age to age.

We use to bury our people, carve a cross, play Mozart's Requiem,
they started a new era of solitude
and loss,
their corpses our trees, our roads,

tones of blood evaporating in the air we breathe,
corpses lost in the tide of all times, high tide
on our empty beach, the grave

we don't deserve, the thoughts we never thought.
Most of you don't even know why and for whom you are crying,
don't see their faces, don't hear their trumpets

when they happen to pass by your door.

Burning Wood As We Talk

I saw it   black shoes tiny overall shadows growing right
from the hair
a bit of light on the left   half child half dream

I found myself in a remote town   the picture is history
but history failed
a picture   I am impressed by my ghostly head my wrongness
my smallness compared to the tree

above
to the house a terra-cotta stove inside burning wood as we talk and sit
on those chairs the flying chairs in the dark   I can be there for
centuries
unmoved

three windows and a pipe facing reality
I smiled   *smiling*   still a word but knowledge fails
surroundings move away   a word that wanders around us
the view slips elsewhere

time doesn't fit in two hands two legs suitcases hours

jump live or die rules in my head are playing ping-pong with the stars

Rough Winter, Cold Meals

It's snowing, freezing, cold meals, shorter days,
people get disoriented, scream, hide,
go to war, die.

Someone on top, on the roof, the basement
full of water, the flood.
Amen, I hear a voice from above.

My husband and I we came from a foreign country,
our pictures too dark, our clothes still unpacked.

Or maybe we never arrived...

There are times when voices are filled with rage.

There are times when the rain is red.

There are times when you are a woman and you think
somewhere in the room there should be a place
where I could hide

a place where I will never die.

History

a chair and a window
the rain
you

take your turn
take into account the room the light
your face like sliding in a ditch

the edge of something scattered moves to the edge
words are ecstatic
the day rustles

the phone rings and goes into history
so does the picture of the two boys
on the beach

dusk falls on earth and all you have to say
fits into the eagle's eye
ready for another rotation

Life Syndrome

what I say is dead wrong
who I am is a mistake

are you here? remember, we are born the same day same hour same mother same
father   who gives directions who chooses the day

blink
I blink
smile
I smile

people think I don't even exist how can I prove you are not me, how can I kill you
with your hand,
this is what confuses me, the lack of rules, the sky too big
the kind of heart rushing to catch my breath -
everything in one direction, one lousy dream...

numbers and leaves to rake

raking the leaves
dear you, I found myself wearing your coat and your shoes

Mouth Without Face

I am again in the dark seasons run out of time the feeling
of that train leaving the station
I am not there

trying to reshape my mouth the lipstick in my purse
no escape
he grabbed my hand spat on the floor
the man without face

I am so patient my poem is not I mean waking up
today
I named it

Berryman Style

and he took a plunge into the world
of sounds
looking for his name head and legs close
to Earth
the ocean blue in one eye   Friday afternoon
on crowded streets
highways new hemispheres ready
to explode

clouds
city of falling gods
love and sex on vacant spaces state of emergency
and all the dust —
he looked around   his other eye open
all of the sudden
leaves us with the question
was he still alive

The Orange Long Tail Story

It comes so fast to my mind the orange
Long tail story limping like
The half moon

Over people in an orange town far away
In the mountains

Where to pray in this desert of hands   if God
Happens dogs also will bite

Have a place in my heart
I slip into a puddle of sounds as the story unfolds

Wings of time

My last punishment

Gravity

I like long titles and short hair the letter B
the birds the balloons

I like my evening dress all silk all red   to walk
along the lake to look around   the rain the ballet

on the roof
I like to pee in the cornfield and think about

new continents brewing in secrecy I like
some other things

the sky at twilight and morning sleep

they could meet in the middle of the page
never falling apart

one rule a day
one planet at a time

News From My Backyard

we are together, right?

the feeling comes from the leaves
yellow and red
all the same in our eyes

from our late shadows beating their wings
against the sun

a moving figure of life

and echoes of *I love you* carried by the wind -

being alive
here at this hour

*

who created the world -

I promise you to make a small change

one word I will whisper
in your ear

even if the wind will take it away and you'll never
hear it:

this is how silence sounds in my yard

love

music

*

I lie down and look at the sky

such a waste of blue and red

I see my thoughts rising   they go around fly
then stop
make in the dark little holes for the stars:

the way crickets are burying silence

*

first it was a sound
then a shape moved in the grass

it scared me

it took me along:

old bones carried away by clouds

Before Dawn

I take the stand in front of you,
my body, old tree,
grown from an undisclosed time.
Sky pours around like jazz,

a festival of stars between two ribs
talking to each other the sweet language
of ashes. Fall comes to my mind:
wandering in my mother's eyes,

green first, then yellow, then red,
keeping up with the music,
the branches, the wood burning inside.
Inside of inside, me too, like a vulture.

My mother opens her eyes,
the music stops, the planet bleeds,
my image staggers in disarray.
Pain comes later with the body,

a word I can't spell.

In Small Waves

1.
Fall is here, the music is gone,
count the dead birds, look for someone you love.

I have no memories of writing letters to you,
the postcard all wrinkled still in my purse.

Thick and muddy the night covers the floor.

2.
Over and over rolling the sun onto the beach, seagulls like us
cross the land in despair.

One boat is leaving, another one in full speed
approaches the shore.

We are due for love.

We move in small waves.

Deep Blue

that day

in the garden we bloomed into bushes of sounds
flashy pink white

deep blue remembering the sea

early spring
patches of snow on the ground melting away

dreams

by surprise
like an old rotten house silence

collapsed

dear mother
the mirror kept me prisoner for so long

I got new eyes new legs
I am coming home

Imagine

After Magritte's *The Use of Words I*

Ceci n'est pas une pipe
The horse waits at the door   then the apple

Flat sounds   spring when the spring comes   birds
When you see one

Magritte's mind as a sea   get to the bottom you'll be naked
You'll lose your name

What is not said and what is over said

The unknown language of our gods   Imagine
What you can't imagine and then what you can

Walking on Earth with several sounds in your mouth
A pipe tattooed on your chest

And I see the carver sharpening his knife

Our chance to be spelled in absence like angels

Playing Ophelia

I write for you, I drag you in this line,
In the space I have I rush you, I cover you
With letters, connect you

To the title.
I write because I can't touch you,
I was at the gate and you didn't come, I wasn't there

And you came with flowers,
I called your name, nobody answered. Night comes
With a loud scream vomiting stars.

I hate the way you are not here
Wearing your black shirt, the way I whisper your name
Without sound.

Let me exit, my hair scares me, the stage is full of rats,
My thoughts are old, older than me.
Give me back the fog, the loneliness, the body I forgot

In your cheap dream.

Blues

and days of burning nights freeze under my skin
and nights of slow birthing and I have to pick you up
from the sea and cradle you and give you
a name

and tell you the story of some red leaves falling
like kisses oh, no,
I surrendered my lips to a man of wind and dust,
I walk on the street playing this old tune

dying for the first time

The Smell Of Snow Reminds

the smell of snow reminds me of a remote town
legs tightened up to the ground
with cold unspoken words

light thin behind the house
an old song -

reminds me of trespassing the hospital gate
tears in a white cup
where someone

breathing not breathing pushed me away
to the other side
of the world

Monday morning

the sun was rising

Sushi Bar

the entire winter my hands were frozen on Chicago

cold streets

three times I wrote this   *I bought woolen gloves*

the letters never arrived

a war going on overseas   my parents are waiting

dazzling on the blue balcony

*

the sushi bar still open   late night   signs of spring

a city alive

yellow cabs   a punk waiter two sakis

an arrangement of eel stars seaweed on a white plate

he says bonjour   the heat is on I look in the mirror

I see me smiling

It's about healing wounds

Five Fingers And No Stars

the night pushed me away from the main road to Michigan state
spring inside the trees   hands mixed with the dark

music on top
five fingers and no stars   a lonely car on the road
a road to everywhere in the world

fog instead of space
time running out of memories   feel the distance
to the next hour   then click

your cell phone lights up

maybe there is an answer maybe there is not

Vallejo's Black Heralds

Vallejo's black heralds

all day around —

wondering if God

had thought

to punish us with such

unbearable

beauty

Lake Triptych

1.
It's me
moving on the verge of what you see

unbalanced like a feather

so nude
the veil torn apart

this is what makes the lake to arouse : eyes

: clouds

white version of human lust

2.
Blue is the color of my thoughts
when red sleeps on the couch

when I can't find my black sun glasses —
and something else you can't see or touch

there is always a large blue shroud on which all corpses are pink

3.
I am in love with the seagull who pecked out my eyes

I stand in front of every sea in the world

I can take everyone's name

I can draw a circle on wet sand

And pretend it's your face

What Remains

1.
And I move again from here to there,
one step ahead of you, exhaling like the ocean
on the hot summer sand.

For moving keeps me in place,
clean and beautiful. Keeps me from being who I am.

Evening sits still in front of me like a porcelain vase.
All birds sleep on the branch

Faces like ours fill up the empty space.

2.
To be there is what takes me here. I want to live
and then I want to die.

I see a squirrel crossing the street, I remember myself on a day
like that, the smell of spring,
a fresh gooseberry

crushed in my mouth.
Fierce words are seizing our children, our trees. What remains
doesn't speak.

I am stuck in the middle of a thought:
happiness, what is your name?

Wild Geese

If I say Monday the clock explodes I am old
And it's Tuesday
I am speeding I pass you I feed you
I crush you
I am flushing you out blowing letters
Around
A film of sounds covers the sky a flock of wild
Geese passes by

My breath keeps the planet afloat the eyes
Are doing the rowing
I am flat and thin between pages
Of time
Fumes from the dead keep giving me directions

Sunday No Mail

Sunday no mail   news comes from wherever
the TV burned away my last neighbor died last fall

nothing dramatic under the ground if I open the window
wind blows leaves   my father speaks

the mind refuses small changes

I am still here so much of everything

Eventually I can move my hand and the shadow
will follow

Like Night And Day

There is a blind girl inside of me
She cries and begs me to let her out

To let her walk on sunny streets and talk to people
And buy things

I see her sometimes in a musical way
Filling the spot I was just leaving

Like night and day

Her hands a crucifix imploring me

But I am speechless I have no words
To call her name

No light
To make a pair of eyes

The Long Hour

still *here*
I couldn't move pass the line

like a saint in the picture both feet on Earth
that roundness
smaller than a soccer ball

still *now*
a solid rock   it rolls and it rolls

I wanted to prove my existence to you
still unproved

and the long hour
minute after minute all suicidal

except the last one I am hanging on

Civility

The vending machine is broken and the sun fell asleep.
Highways go nowhere, people are deaf.

I ought to die but the mortician won't take me,
he can't dig in / out a corpse or a can

the vending machine is broken, it has to be fixed,
so we can drink milk and talk to the stars, hey,

I don't know how to be a child, help me wind,
help me time.

Rain raining no snack no rainbow on the way to school.

I am wearing black.

The Day I Missed

The web of hours hangs loose

I could have come closer to the window,
ball of light
eye within eyes

the view pivots and widens

the city through half-closed blinds
scatters thoughts in the sky

I should probably cover that lamp
bring home the blue mountains

my feet are cold shadows

I keep stepping on dead reptiles

When Blue Goes Wrong

when blue goes wrong what can we do
dogs are barking poets are dying

the *blue guitar* is just a mop —
mopping up and mopping down

what's wrong with us

we open big mouths like big fish left on the shore

*

hard to breathe
let's try the snow the red the blush
the blues
sue Monet for his lack of black

talk more?   talk less?   or leave it to the stars

they might dig us out

Insomnia In Flowers

I was walking on a narrow dim wonderful
small road

stepping on rocks looking for answers

I went to the edge of one thing

I found nothing

my house floats backwards on the river

a child in the garden opens
black wings

*

who should be here

whom do I speak

who lost his tooth in the green of the ocean —

I dip my hands in the night

nobody starts crying

*

don't talk

insomnia in flowers

a blue silhouette that could fit in my dream

what I can't bear any longer

the smell of the moon

the music of untitled poems

Winter Talk

love is a ghost   let it inside   welcome

the winter

don't talk listen   dress it in white:

the empty space between day and night

*

finish the sentence

the first drop of rain is yours

days like hawks hover around

souls yet unborn adjust their wings
haunting the body

*

the clouds look at me   a song in the snake's
yellow tongue

but I don't hear don't see them or

vice-versa

I could see at once the eye and the clouds

ball of fire   from uncollected ashes:
a hymn

to stones and flowers dead sisters old friends

the rain will wash out the pain

*

to enter your memory: like flirting with death

coming to the conclusion of wearing pale colors light shoes

hiking the clouds

digging a tomb I will never fall

inside
where nobody pays attention

*

rarely I understand what I am saying
part of the meaning goes to leaves part to the tree

and what are they saying about me   another
mother tongue

a pantomime
this is how all things started   a landscape with teeth

I want to lie down in the snow with no stars above

If you come to me with one more word...

*

the mind wears black not knowing why

one little hour sits in my hand

I see you coming with the storm of years

curtains flow crimson (color of your sky)

windows go drunk   I see you tall   I see you running

sleeveless like ready to lift me up

Roots Go Beyond The Sky

Roots go beyond the sky   humans
Think of the next spring

Heart upon heart the language of corpses

A flower in the mouth
Teeth coupling with stars

Roots up and down brought us in the middle
Of a phrase

Between two sounds
Which one of these words will die

I would rather skip the end

Love At Dusk Or How To Deal With Bad Weather

Dusk threatens me with dark colors and deadly sounds.
I am ready to be, to belong to my name.

Your touch vanishes. Earth recessed for the night.

We used to name things, clouds, so they could be,
Move, stay...

Fierce as the moon a last minute God descends
And I become silence.

A rainy face in memory of wind.
Vowels fell first, long stormy legs, a missing body.

Winter Talk (2)

so much a room into room a shadow dragging my feet
a snowflake on the tip of the tongue
a souvenir

so much terror in flowers let's open the windows
talk about spring wait
for the postman

to come
let's trim the night set up the scene
for those

who want to return on Earth

Sweet Amnesia

I am on my way to the door

Open it

It's open he said and closed his eyes morning came

And the sun

Blinds me   people run out of food

Out of time

They don't remember don't talk don't rush

They are missing their turn

To something better cheaper more beautiful...

I forgot the names of all the birds   if they want to fly

How are they going not to

Who killed first and lasted for ever?

Here Again In The Mist

1.
here again in the mist stealing words
from your mouth

soaked in our dreams
I am the perfect thief you are the perfect corpse
Our savior told us nothing

2.
big ideas deserted me long time ago so I force myself
into small places
holes
closets
drawers
days

death is O.K. but this obsession with life...

A Process In The Weather Of The Heart

    Or

        Sunday At The Beach Learning Foreign Languages

> " A process in the weather of the heart
> Turns damp to dry; the golden shot
> Storms in the freezing tomb."
>   Dylan Thomas

1.
I put on my sunglasses to look like
when I was twelve.

Romanian time. They were digging out a corpse,
A drowned man.

From that brutal silence.

He was covered with weeds, shells, swollen, black.
Children around were playing the ball.

The horizon.

A dark blue line.

Storm on everyone's face.

2.
I bought a beer at the end of the deck.
I sent postcards to my friends. Red umbrellas, women
With big hats, ecstasy in the air.

The horizon came closer.

The corpse deflated.

Time filled with sand.

3.
I am still learning the language of death.

That Piece Of Art Next To The Snow

and I said bring the light closer to my eyes
the flash-light the hand

piece of art next to the snow

the blue thing   taking shape
by the river

a floating mind

*

Our boat still leaves

Shall we go further or stop between trees

Vanish at down

Daily Green

we change ideas about colors and facts
and suddenly stop breathing

you liked green   green is gone
it might come back

but you won't see it
how can I explain to you...

the world if flat
except a small mound on top

we call it life

It Takes A Song

I have the courage to say *no* —
Yes breaks my heart in many ways
It's sticky hot hangs on my eyes delight
And fear makes me cry

Makes me snow too far away
From where I live
Strange places —

It snows in the room time spreading
In waves

It takes a song to breathe again
Wait
You are supposed not to be here
I dumped you dead
One day

Yes

When...

Sunday No Mail (2)

frozen news   the night expands

extinct volcano

magma

I want to turn on the light the gesture

doesn't reach the hand

*

the ocean flaps in my face   salt and memories

a house burns on both sides
of Earth

a tiny envelop floats on waves
heading undisturbed

to nowhere

On Turtles And Death

nothing told me that I will soon die

my hands are in place

my legs

the book in front of me breezy

waves brewing time

from the heart a bric-a-brac of old
toys   nothing to be stored

on the other side

I live in secrecy   don't call my name

*

in my dream I was a turtle with blue eyes

rolling my shell in exotic waters

death like a twister

I dragged myself out of the sea

my black sisters the pearls conspire

against me

distort the limbs

new ritual of hiding   deepest

layers

invention of speech

*

the high tide leaves more verbs on the beach

I drew them all over my feet   *they whisper*

I am on my knees

an exercise in leaning   hand written letters

for tall priests

Descartes would love to see me naked

Chinese leaves are good

for depression

one verb hanged on the page

cold the brain half-aware

*

final poem? maybe   from the transparency to the idea

of earth

bodies   hearts   more tongues than sounds

one life is worth several deaths

I share with you the light of this Monday morning

Could be the final thought of the day

*

I am your landscape of death my lover you

your whole picture in the room

the skull of life well crafted well hanged

in four golden nails

The Red Window

the window was red
the house full of unexpected guests
impossible like reaching the sea
our steps on the moving floor

through the red one can sleep
dream of the green of your
green shadow — a tree
you never planted in your yard

then came the time for the red
to be white
to be meaningless
a time when I was wearing

my belongings for the night
I was ready to die

I Am Not The Rainbow

I am not the rainbow you see shining
down-hill

purple   dark blue   antique
a touch of white:

      clarity while changing
the guard
two heralds our friends and so quiet the place

no words could ever reach my lips   so far from you
as in a dream

I am not the rainbow not yet in the sky as winter
approaches with all

its dust
here again in my yard looking for my shawl of dark

Sunset

Where should I go to see another sunset,
No vessels leaving the shore, no funerals.

It happened at once on a small scale of change,
Disappearance into disappearance,
Elements sleeping like strangers one next to the other.

The swan crosses the hour.

Someone at the end should have been
As human as the night which descends
Without expectations, without a knife.

What you told me in front of the house,
Who you were then with your warm wet hands
Of desire
All went back into waves: stone, shell.

Pieces of history standing inside demolition.

The next sunset is what we are longing for,
We, who were born in this slow elation of time,
Nothing else could have happened to us.

Fish Scales

fish scales to be removed with a knife on the big kitchen table
moon music
somebody swallows the shadow

a woman in her early age removed from our time her pink suit
hangs in the closet

we drive we don't look back we have to catch our breath   the road
leaves the town

birds on their way South

some light remains untouched

If Nowhere

if nowhere is here where does the space
start
the town in which I could built
a house
and then hang up the windows

to stop thinking it takes years
time expands
beyond
time   not too friendly
the stars

and the blind eagle rows away taking
along our landscape: *the mind shivers*
what exists not to be seen

Intermission

and all the roads took us to the Black Sea
always before dawn   the sand
still wet
seagulls sleeping in the air

where is everyone you once asked
and looked around

one by one the stars were leaving the world
we were leaving our bodies

each moment postponed to eternity

it was long before time

About the Author

Stella Vinitchi Radulescu, born in **Romania**, is the author of several collections of poetry published in the United States, Romania and **France**, including *My Dream Has Red Fingers (2000)*, *From Heaven with Love (2003)*, *Self Portrait in Blue (2004)*, *Last Call (2005)*, *Terre Interrompue*, winner of 2007 Grand Prize "Art & Poésie" International Competition and *Un Cri dans la Neige*, Grand Prix Noël-Henri Villard 2008.

She has had poems in *Seneca Review, California Quarterly, Karamu, White Pelican, Shade (Anthology), Pleiades, Louisville Review,* as well as in a variety of literary magazines in France, **Belgium, Luxembourg, Quebec** and Romania. She is a lecturer in French at Northwestern University.

www.ingramcontent.com/pod-product-compliance
Lightning Source LLC
Chambersburg PA
CBHW071840290426
44109CB00017B/1884